Biomes

Rainforests

Tony Allan

Chrysalis Children's Books

BIOMES

DESERTS
GRASSLANDS
OCEANS
RAINFORESTS
WETLANDS

Produced by Monkey Puzzle Media Ltd
Gissing's Farm, Fressingfield, Suffolk IP21 5SH, UK

First published in the UK in 2003 by
Ⓒ Chrysalis Children's Books
64 Brewery Road, London N7 9NT

A Belitha Book

Editor: JohnWoodward
Editorial Manager: Joyce Bentley
Designer: Mark Whitchurch
Consultant: Michael Allaby
Picture Researcher: Glass Onion Pictures

ISBN: 1 84138 871 8

British Library Cataloguing in Publication Data for this book is available from
the British Library.

Printed in Hong Kong / China
10 9 8 7 6 5 4 3 2 1

Picture Acknowledgements
We wish to thank the following individuals and organizations for their help and
assistance, and for supplying material in their collections: Digital Vision *front cover*, 5 top;
Ecoscene 41 (Wayne Lawler); Papilio 16 (Robert Pickett); Edward Parker 11, 13, 14, 22, 26,
27, 28 bottom, 28–29, 31, 34, 38, 40, 43, 44, 46–47; Science Photo Library 30 ((NRSC Ltd);
South American Pictures 4 (Bill Leimbach); Still Pictures 1 (Jany Sauvenet), 3 (Michael
Sewell), 5 middle (Dominique Halleux), 5 bottom (Mark Edwards), 6 (Andre Bartschi),
8–9 (Carsten Rahbek), 9 top (Kevin Schafer), 10 (Alan Watson), 12 (Juan Carlos Munoz),
17 (Michael Sewell), 18 (Jany Sauvenet), 19 (Andre Bartschi), 20 (Nigel Dickinson), 21
(Nigel Dickinson), 23 (Mark Edwards), 24 (Edward Parker), 25 (Walter Hodge), 32 top
(Tantyo Bangun), 32–33 (John Maier), 35 (Mark Edwards), 36–37 (Gerard and Margi
Moss), 37 top (Cyril Ruoso), 39 (Art Wolfe), 42 (Fred Bruemmer), 45 (Ron Giling), 47 top
(Giles Nicolet). Artwork by Michael Posen. The pictures used in this book do not show
the actual people named in the case studies in the text.

The author acknowledges the help of Dr Marcus Colchester, of the World Rainforest
Movement, in preparing the text for this volume.

CONTENTS

Zeca's World

The world that Zeca inhabits has changed little in thousands of years. A 15-year-old living in the Amazon rainforest, she belongs to the Yanomami people, who occupy a vast belt of almost uninterrupted woodland near the Brazil-Venezuela border. Her days are spent in and around the yano, the ring-shaped communal house that she and her parents share with a dozen other families.

'THE RAINFOREST IS our home, the only one we know. It gives us all we need – food to eat, medicines when we are sick, wood and palm fronds to build the yano. We grow cotton to make the aprons and waistbands that we wear, and there's a forest plant called urucu that provides the red dye we paint on our faces and bodies to make ourselves look beautiful. We use brightly-coloured flowers and feathers to adorn our heads and arms, and shells from the riverside to make necklaces.

Days are mostly like one another, except for the special times when we go to a neighbouring yano for a feast. I wake with the sun, but there's no rush to get up; maybe I'll eat some papaya fruit, and then get back into the hammock until the family are up and about. Most days I go to the gardens with my mother to help with the weeding, and we make trips out into the forest where she shows me which wild fruit and berries are good to eat. She has taught me everything I know: how to thread necklaces, where to find crabs and crayfish by the riverside, how to make bread from the vegetable called manioc.

Yet my mother seems worried. The other adults talk of the foreigners who have come with huge machines to cut down trees not far from our village. They brought diseases with them, which killed some Yanomami in a nearby yano. We hope they don't come here. They would spoil everything.'

Conflicting claims

The rainforests were once the exclusive territory of indigenous peoples like the Yanomami, but now millions of people worldwide have an interest in them.

LOGGERS
Loggers like this worker in an Indonesian forest can earn a living for a time by cutting down the giant forest trees for timber or processing into woodpulp. But once the trees are gone, the loggers are out of a job – and the forest may have been destroyed.

FARMERS
Settlers, like this farmer in Madagascar, seek to make new lives for themselves by farming plots of land cleared from the rainforest. Yet they often find that the forest soil is not suitable for growing crops in the long term, and have to abandon their farms.

PLANTATION WORKERS
Employees on managed plantations can earn a more secure living by producing sustainable forest products. This worker is tapping a rubber tree for its sap, or latex. The wound on the tree bark will heal, and the latex will be turned into rubber.

What Are Rainforests?

Covering about one-twentieth of the earth's land surface, the rainforests form a wooded belt around the tropics. They are places with high, regular rainfall, where the hot, damp conditions encourage many different species of trees and plants to grow. For the part they play in keeping the world green, they have been called the lungs of the planet.

Not far from its source in Peru, the River Amazon winds its way through the rainforest in a series of giant loops, or meanders.

THE LOWLAND RAINFOREST of West Africa can seem one of the most inhospitable places on the planet. One way of visiting the forest is by boat, travelling up one of the wide rivers that drain the tropical rainfall from the land. The hot, moist, sunlit banks of the river offer ideal growing conditions, and trees and other plants press down to the water's edge on both banks. They form such a dense, unbroken tangle of vegetation that landing and travelling through the forest on foot seems impossible. From the boat, it looks like the jungle of myths and legends: a place of mystery, extreme discomfort and danger.

Yet the true rainforest is not like this. In the heart of the forest there is no tangle of vegetation, because almost no direct sunlight reaches the ground to stimulate growth. Instead there are just the trunks of massive trees, soaring almost branchless 50m up to the forest canopy. Here they finally spread out, parasol-like, to catch the sun's rays. Animals are all around, in the uppermost branches and in the leaf litter underfoot, but they are mostly silent and difficult to spot. The atmosphere is cathedral-like, with the tree trunks resembling the great churches' rearing columns of stone. It is beautiful, and not in the least threatening. But it is still rainforest.

Technically, rainforests are areas of woodland that receive more than 150–200 cm of rain a year. The rainfall is spread throughout the year; there is no really dry season, even if some months are wetter than others.

Most rainforest lies in the tropics, but there are also rainforests in many cooler parts of the globe: in New Zealand, Tasmania, China, southern Japan, on the Pacific coast of North America and in parts of the southeastern USA. These temperate rainforests differ in several important ways from the tropical forests. They have a wider range of soils, but fewer tree species. The decomposition of dead plant and animal material is slower in the cooler climate, so the forest floor is thick with leaf litter and humus.

The tropical rainforests lie in a wide belt stretching around the Equator. They cover four major areas: the tropics of Central and South America; Central Africa; Southeast Asia, from India through Malaysia and Thailand to the Philippines and Indonesia; and northeastern Australia and the neighbouring island of New Guinea.

As shown by the bright green areas on the map, the world's tropical rainforests form a belt around the Equator that crosses four continents.

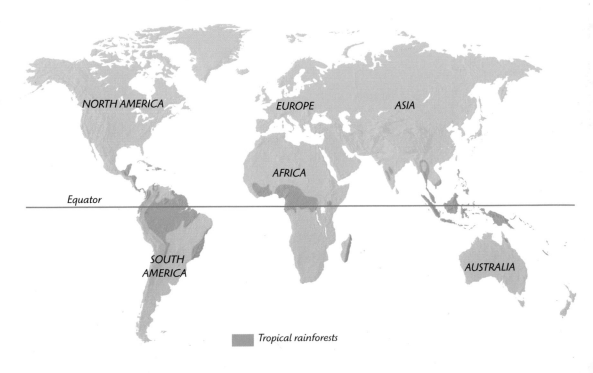

NORTH AMERICA

EUROPE

ASIA

AFRICA

Equator

SOUTH AMERICA

AUSTRALIA

Tropical rainforests

What are the main types of rainforests?

Scientists divide the world's tropical rainforests into many different varieties. Primary lowland forest – the cathedral type – is generally found at altitudes below 1000m. It has the widest range of different plant and animal species, and the tallest trees. Often the canopy may be more than 50m above ground level. Some giant trees grow even higher; the tallest broadleaf tree ever recorded was a species found in lowland forest in Sarawak (part of Malaysia) that measured 83m. By comparison, the world's tallest tree, a Californian redwood, is 112m tall.

What is a biome?

A biome is a major regional community of plants and animals, with similar life forms and environmental conditions. Each biome is named after its dominant feature, such as tropical rainforest, grassland, or coral reef.

Montane forest begins at altitudes of 1000–1500m. Because of the extra height above sea level, temperatures are cooler, and the moisture in the air frequently turns to mist, obscuring the sun's rays. The trees are shorter, and do not need the huge buttress roots that are a feature of many lowland forest trees. Clinging to hillsides where water would otherwise run off rapidly, these forests play a vital part in stopping flash floods.

Higher up still lies cloud forest, where the mists of the montane forests turn to almost perpetual cloud. These are damp, gloomy, green places, where the trees themselves are cloaked in ferns, and the branches droop under the weight of mosses and lichens. Animals are relatively scarce, although the central African cloud forest is famously the home of the mountain gorillas, of which only about 600 now remain.

Above the cloud forest is elfin forest: a ghostly landscape of gnarled, stunted trees hardly taller than a man. This represents the rainforest's last gasp before it gives way to the sparse vegetation of the mountain tops.

A mature rainforest tree soars up towards the sunlight in a Costa Rican forest. Its huge roots not only soak up whatever moisture is available, but also bind the soil together and provide shelter for smaller plants and a wide variety of tropical insects.

At high altitude the Andes mountains of Ecuador are covered with cloud forest. It is hard for vegetation to take root on these steep slopes, and the trees are shorter than in lowland forest.

Specially adapted to grow in muddy, salty estuaries, mangroves stretch out prop roots on the Indonesian island of Sumatra.

Are all tropical forests true rainforests?

Other types of tropical forest share many of the features of true rainforest. Areas of sandy soil in the lowlands support heath forest. Here the trees are shorter and slower-growing than those in primary rainforest, because they do not enjoy such damp conditions. They have to find ways of getting extra water from the dry earth, and some have wide-spreading 'root-mats' to suck up every last drop of moisture from the area round their trunks.

Conditions could hardly be more different in swamp forests, which are either flooded for part of the year during the wet season, or waterlogged all year round. Here the trees must be able to tolerate the floods or risk drowning like overwatered plants.

Another special case is the mangrove forest that often merges with coastal rainforest, carrying the tree cover beyond the tideline and out into the sea itself. The world's most extensive mangrove forest covers the Sundarbans swamp region in the Ganges delta on the Bangladesh-India border, but mangroves are also found in Central and South America, Southeast Asia and Australia.

Despite these differences, all these tropical forests have a lot in common with true rainforest. They are hot and damp, shaded from direct sunlight by the cover of the leaves. Usually they are drained by many rivers that carry rainwater back to the sea. Being close to the Equator, they are places where day and night are of roughly equal length. Above all they are rich in life – not just in greenery, but in insects, reptiles, birds and mammals. These animals live by either eating the forest vegetation or by preying upon each other.

Fan palms flourish in a forest clearing in Cape Tribulation National Park, Queensland – one of the few surviving patches of Australian rainforest.

The Australian rainforest

Covering just 10 500 sq. km of the northeastern state of Queensland, Australia's rainforest is relatively small. Even so, it contains many ancient plants found nowhere else on earth. They include huge, slow-growing kauri pines, some of them more than 1000 years old, and the vine-like magnolia known as *Austrobaileya scandens*, thought to be the world's oldest surviving flowering plant species.

The forest also shelters a unique community of animals, including marsupials such as tree kangaroos, forest wallabies, possums, bandicoots, cuscuses and quolls. In the past, some of the area was cleared by ranchers, farmers and loggers, but since 1988 most of the surviving forest has been protected as a World Heritage Site.

What Grows In Rainforests?

Left to themselves, rainforests are the most unchanging places on Earth. Beneath the tree canopy the weather is hot and humid, and in the oldest rainforests it has been so for the past 60 million years. So it is scarcely surprising that there are more different types of plant in these tropical hothouses than anywhere else on the planet.

NOWHERE ELSE ON Earth has so many kinds of life as the rainforest. In temperate lands, a patch of woodland may typically have between 25 and 75 different species of tree per hectare, but the figure for tropical forest is between 250 and 500 different species. Scientists surveying a single patch of rainforest covering just 2.5 sq. km near the headwaters of the River Amazon found that it contained more flowering plant species than the whole of Britain.

The richness of plant life in the rainforest is linked to the explosive speed with which the vegetation grows. Even trees, which elsewhere inch slowly from the soil, shoot upward in the damp heat; some smaller varieties can put on as much as 2.5m in a year. They can do so because they have a constant supply of warmth and moisture, the essential conditions for growth.

Glowing red in the sun, bromeliads cluster on a tree in the Peruvian rainforest. The plants hitch a lift towards the sun by growing high above the forest floor on tree trunks and branches.

Even so, there are limits to the forest's generosity. Little direct sunlight penetrates the high canopy of leaves. Worse still, the soil usually contains relatively few nutrients, the vital minerals that plants need to grow. The result is a fierce competition in which only the plants best suited to the particular conditions can hope to survive. The fact that those conditions constantly vary from place to place, if only in tiny details, helps explain why the rainforest has so many species. Each one is a specialist at surviving in its own tiny corner of the forest.

What types of plants grow best?

Certain types of plant flourish better in the rainforest than anywhere else. These include tropical hardwood trees such as mahogany and teak, which defend themselves against insects and damp by developing extremely dense wood that is rich in resins and other protective chemicals. It is this very toughness that makes hardwoods so valuable to woodworkers in the developed world, and makes logging in the rainforest such a profitable business. If the felled trees were rapidly replaced by younger ones there would be no problem, but tropical hardwoods are exceptionally slow-growing by rainforest standards. A tree cut down in minutes with a chainsaw may take hundreds of years to replace.

Taking advantage of the trees to hitch a lift up to the sunlight are thousands of creepers. Nine out of ten of all the climbing plants found in gardens come from the rainforest. Vines and woody lianas wrap themselves around the trunks in a desperate struggle upwards. Strangest of all are the many epiphytes that cling to the trees. These plants have no roots, but instead draw all the water that they need from the rain or the air around them, and all their nutrients from the soil that eventually forms on the broader branches of the trees themselves.

Corkscrewing towards the light, a liana wraps itself around a tree trunk in the Amazon rainforest. Such strangler vines can kill their host trees.

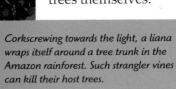

Is there order in the chaos?

At first sight the teeming plant life of the forest may seem chaotic, but it has an order of its own. Rainforests grow in layers, each with its own typical plant life. At the top is the canopy, where the high trees spread their leaves and the most successful lianas and epiphytes burst into flower. Below, at maybe half the height, is the understorey, made up of smaller tree species or giants that have still to grow to their full height. Some three to five metres above the forest floor is a layer of undergrowth made up of shrubby plants, often with many stems in place of a single trunk.

Robbed of sunlight by all the greenery above it, the forest floor itself is surprisingly clear of vegetation. Instead, a rich crop of fungi takes advantage of everything that falls from the upper reaches, and recycles the nutrients that are released as the leaves and branches decay. Fungi are not plants, and do not need sunlight to survive, so they can flourish in the gloom of the forest floor.

In places where trees have fallen, the high canopy is broken. The young saplings get enough light to complete their growth, rising rapidly to fill the gap in the canopy. Only where large areas have been felled does real chaos reign. In these patches of 'secondary-growth forest', plants of all kinds struggle for the precious sunlight, leading to the development of impenetrable thickets.

These vegetation battlegrounds are not at all typical of true rainforest, but they often develop at the forest edge, where visitors are most likely to see them. It was because of these thickets that the rainforest came to be viewed as impassable jungle – a reputation that it lost only slowly as people came to understand it better.

The highest trees in a typical rainforest may break through to form an open 'emergent' layer.

The crowns of most of the big trees form an almost continuous layer about 25m above the ground, called the canopy.

Halfway down to the ground from the forest canopy is the understorey, formed of smaller or half-grown trees.

Near the forest floor a layer of shrubby undergrowth struggles to survive in the dim light.

Helping out

Many rainforest plants and animals have formed alliances that help them survive. Scientists call them 'symbiotic' relationships, from a Greek word meaning 'living together'. A good example of this is the association between fig plants and wasps.

Fig flowers are hidden inside fig fruits, and rely on fig-wasps to bring the pollen they need to set seeds. Each flower produces a scent to attract a female wasp, which burrows into the hard fruit. The wasp buries her eggs in the pulpy insides, where the ripening fruit will provide food and shelter for her growing young. But in return she has carried the vital pollen into the flower on her body, and this enables the fig to breed as well.

What Lives In Rainforests?

People who visit rainforests are often surprised by how few animals they can see. Yet all around them the forest is teeming with life. From the leaf litter to the canopy, different creatures – centipedes and ants, as well as mammals, birds, frogs and lizards – make their homes among the trees.

THE FACTORS THAT make the rainforests the earth's richest treasure houses of plant life also enable them to support an amazing number of animals. The constant heat and moisture, the relative absence of seasons, a climate that has changed little for millions of years: all these encourage life to flourish all year round. There is no winter in which food supplies dry up, as there is in colder climes, forcing some creatures to lie dormant for the winter, and others to migrate to places where food is still plentiful. Even if some times of year are more productive than others, there are always leaves and fruit to be

eaten somewhere. They grow in such quantities that an African hornbill can easily gather 200 fruits a day to feed its family in the nest.

The forest supports many cold-blooded animals such as snakes and frogs, which rely on the sun's heat to maintain their body temperature. The steady warmth means that they can be active throughout the day and night, rather than just by day as they are in colder parts of the world. And because of the regular availability of food, animals can breed at all times of year, rather than only in certain seasons.

Insects thrive in the hot, damp conditions of the rainforest. These young grasshoppers are clustering on leaves near the forest floor in Belize, Central America.

A jaguar visits a forest pool in Amazonia. Big hunters are relatively rare in the rainforest, for want of suitable prey.

Why are there so many types of animals?

The different layers of the rainforest offer animals a wide variety of places to live, and ways to find food. As a result there is a much greater diversity of creatures than in less favoured biomes. A single large tree can shelter as many as 50 different species of creatures, while 90 species of frogs and toads have been counted in one small area of Peruvian rainforest – more than in the entire USA. Insects flourish in these conditions, in such variety that there are probably millions of species still to be discovered.

The peculiar conditions of the rainforest favour some animals more than others. Insects and cold-blooded animals can grow to great sizes: the rainforest is the home of giant anacondas, goliath beetles, bird-eating spiders, giant frogs and giant snails. By contrast there are few big mammals, although elephants inhabit the African and Asian forests, and rhinos were once common in the forests of Malaysia. Above all, large meat-eaters are scarce, apart from a few forest-dwelling tigers and jaguars.

The reason lies in the nature of the food available. While the huge numbers of insects provide food for animals up to the size of anteaters, there is little to tempt big grazing animals like the gazelles, antelope and zebras that live in great herds on the African plains. The hunters that prey on these big, fast-running animals tend to stay out on the plains too, avoiding the forests.

Instead, the rainforests support a wonderful array of creatures that are specially adapted to their own peculiar conditions. In Madagascar there are giraffe-necked weevils, which have heads on stalks to see over the leaf litter. South America has the hoatzin, an ungainly bird with a huge gut that eats vast quantities of leaves. The hoatzin owes its alternative name 'stinkbird' to the smell of cow manure that its leafy diet produces. Sloths, as inactive as their name suggests, only rarely come down from the trees where they feed and mate. Their grappling-hook claws are so strong that their bodies can even remain hanging from the branches for days after their deaths.

DEBATE - Should zoos be used to breed endangered animals?

- Yes. The situation in the rainforests has become so serious that, for many threatened animals, the alternative to captive breeding is extinction.
- No. Wild animals' rightful place is in the forest, not in artificial enclosures. Buying and selling them, whether for zoos or the pet trade, encourages poaching.

What lives where?

Each level of the rainforest has its own particular types of animal life. The forest floor is the realm of the ants, beetles, spiders, scorpions, centipedes, millipedes, worms and woodlice. There they find shelter under the leaf litter or beneath fallen logs, and some burrow deep into the soil. The secondary level of undergrowth provides food for medium-size leaf-eaters: bushpigs in Africa, small deer and wild cattle in Asia, and coatis, capybara and peccaries

The three-toed sloth is a tropical American leaf-eater that spends almost all its life in the trees, hanging from the branches by its big, immensely strong claws.

in the tropical American forests. Here too are the few big hunting animals that prey on these browsers: forest tigers in Asia, and jaguars in America. The gap between the lower levels of the forest and the canopy provides flying space for birds. Some of these sweep through the forest in large mixed flocks that contain as many as 50 different species.

The canopy itself teems with life that is attracted by the fruit and flowers that abound there. Many animals have ingenious adaptations for climbing: the lizards known as geckos have specially-shaped hairs on the pads of their feet that permit them to cling to glossy leaves (and even glass). Tree frogs have discs at the tips of their toes that serve as suction pads. Tree-dwelling anteaters have powerful claws for clinging to branches, and long tongues for raiding the tree nests of termites.

Other animals have dramatic ways of moving from tree to tree. Many monkeys make spectacular leaps, and various squirrels, lemurs, snakes and lizards glide from branch to branch using flaps of skin that can be extended as temporary wings. All around there is life, adapted over millions of years to take advantage of every opportunity for survival that the forest world offers.

A flock of macaws brightens a clearing in the Peruvian Amazon. Their vivid colours are much less conspicuous in the shade beneath the forest canopy.

How Do People Survive In Rainforests?

For thousands of years people have been living in rainforests without harming their surroundings. These native peoples rely on the forest and its wildlife for their food, the clothes they wear and the houses they live in. But over the past century their way of life has been threatened as never before.

The Yanomami hunters of northern Amazonia use very long, powerful bows to bring down animals from high in the forest canopy.

NOBODY KNOWS WHEN people first moved into the world's rainforests. Forest peoples build no stone monuments for archaeologists to dig up and date. Their wooden houses and tools quickly decay in the damp heat, leaving no record behind them. But it is almost certain that the first people moved in many thousands of years ago. At that time – a period long before the development of farming – they survived by a combination of hunting animals and gathering fruits and other foods.

How did the hunter-gatherers live?

There were no herds of big animals for these forest hunter-gatherers to target, as there were on the African plains. Instead, they had to range widely to find enough small game. In central Africa today a single band of Mbuti pygmies, who still live in the African rainforest as hunter-gatherers, typically hunts over as many as 1300 sq. km: an average of about one person for every 4 sq. km. For this reason, the rainforest has never supported large numbers of dedicated hunters.

However, the rivers were full of fish, which people speared or caught in nets made with plant fibres. They also found ways of bringing down animals from the tree-tops, using bows and arrows or darts fired from blowpipes. Their weapons became much more lethal when they started tipping them with poisons taken from plants or – in one part of Amazonia – from the toxic skin of the small tree frogs that are still known as poison-arrow frogs.

The women became expert gatherers, learning where to find rich stores of fruits, nuts and nutritious roots and tubers. People found ways of stealing honey from the nests of wild bees, often using smoke to drive away the angry insects. They also discovered that some forest insects made good food.

The forest proved to be a generous provider. There was always food available, and no one starved. Travelling around in small family groups, the hunter-gatherers developed a lifestyle in which there were no great chiefs or elaborate social ranks. The only people who could claim authority were those whose wisdom or survival skills made them generally respected.

Three generations come together in one longhouse – a large building shared by an extended family in the rainforests of Borneo.

How do native people farm the forest?

Today there are still forest peoples who live entirely as hunter-gatherers, although their numbers are small. Many more prefer to combine some hunting and gathering with a form of farming that is known as shifting cultivation, or slash-and-burn.

Normally the people who support themselves in this way live in temporary villages. They clear a patch of forest around the village, cutting down all but the highest trees, and burn the timber and foliage they have cut down. The ash from the fire is rich in plant nutrients released by burning the wild vegetation. When dug into the soil, the ash makes it fertile enough to grow crops – maybe fruit trees like bananas, or roots like yams or cassava. But the crop plants absorb the nutrients, and after two or three years the soil loses its richness and the crops start to fail.

A rainforest farmer in Africa clears the land using the slash–and–burn technique.

Once the land is cleared, it can be planted with crops. This Sumatran villager is planting petai trees, which produce edible, garlic-flavoured pods. She belongs to the Talang Mamak people, farmers whose way of life is threatened by forest clearance.

The cultivators have no fertilizer that they can add to the soil. So they abandon the old patch, clear another, and start the process all over again. Eventually, after maybe 20 years, when all the land around the community has been used for farming, they may decide to move the entire village and start afresh elsewhere in the forest. Traditional communities are so small compared to the forest area that they can keep doing this indefinitely, and they never have to return to the patches that they have cultivated. So over the years the abandoned, weed-strewn clearings become scrubby 'secondary forest', and then revert to full primary rainforest.

By constantly moving from patch to patch, and leaving the land that they have abandoned to regrow, the indigenous peoples have managed to survive for centuries without doing any permanent damage to the forest and its wildlife. Their lifestyle could hardly be more different from that of developers who come in from outside seeking to clear whole swathes of forests for permanent ranches or plantations. One way of life allows the forest to renew itself; the other destroys it.

The Waorani of Ecuador

Living near the headwaters of the Amazon in Ecuador, the Waorani are a forest tribe of about 1600 people. In the past they were famously fierce, and the neighbouring peoples called them Aucas, or 'savages'. In the 1950s they attracted international attention by spearing to death five missionaries seeking to befriend them. However, the widows of two of the men finally made peaceful contact, and the Waorani were gradually made familiar with the wider world.

Yet the change has not been all for the better. Waorani children now go to school, but what they learn there cuts them off from their traditional way of life without giving them the skills they need to succeed elsewhere. So while the Waorani are joining the modern world, partly by choice, they share very little of its wealth.

Why Does The World Need Rainforests?

Rainforests are important to everyone, not just the people who live in them. They make some of the world's hottest regions moist and green, and without their protection these regions could turn into deserts. They shelter far more than their share of the planet's life, and they may also help keep the world's climate in balance.

RAINFORESTS ARE VITAL to the world because they create flourishing webs of life in regions that would otherwise be desert. Some of the rain that falls on them – more than half of it, according to some studies – never reaches the ground, because it is caught by the upper canopy of leaves. There the raindrops soon evaporate in the heat of the sun's rays, rising into the air in the form of water vapour. This condenses into clouds as it hits cooler air higher up in the atmosphere. The clouds then act as a shield against the drying effects of the sun, and the moisture they contain soon returns to the forest as rain.

The forest, in other words, has its own local water cycle, sustained by the trees themselves; it serves as a rainmaker. Meanwhile, it also collects the rain that does succeed in penetrating the canopy and reaching its lower layers.

Storm clouds loom over the Amazon River. Forest trees soak up excess rainwater, helping to save communities downstream from flooding.

The spreading roots of the great rainforest trees channel and pool rain water as well as soaking it up, acting as very effective barriers against soil erosion.

Some rainwater is caught on the way to the ground by tree foliage, or by the plants known as epiphytes. These plants cling to the branches of trees, where they rely on falling rain and the steamy dampness of the forest for all their water needs. They have no roots of their own, so they cannot draw up moisture from the soil. Many of these plants retain water in cup-like rosettes of overlapping leaves. The pools that form in big epiphytes develop whole little ecosystems of their own. They are breeding grounds for creatures like tree frogs and bromeliad crabs, which live out their entire lives high in the branches.

Rain that does reach the ground is also hoarded by the forest trees. A network of interlocking roots holds it in place, stopping it running off in streams and carrying the thin forest soil away with it. Much of the water is absorbed by the tree roots, and is pumped back up the trees to evaporate from their leaves. The rest seeps away through the ground, but very gradually. This means that the great rivers that drain the forests are fed at the rate of a steady trickle rather than a sudden torrent, as would happen after every tropical storm if it were not for the holding action of the tree roots. So the forest trees also prevent the soil erosion that can easily reduce tropical landscapes to barren wastelands.

Soil erosion

One study in the Ivory Coast region of West Africa showed that the loss of soil from forested slopes was just 30 kg per hectare a year. That's the equivalent of 30 standard bags of sugar. But on hillsides where the tree cover had been removed, soil erosion during tropical rainstorms multiplied the rate of soil loss by almost 2000, to a staggering 138 tonnes – the equivalent of about 100 average family cars.

How do rainforests affect climate?

In addition to their local effects, the rainforests also affect the climate of the Earth as a whole, in ways that are still not fully understood. Like all green plants, the forest trees use carbon dioxide to make sugars and other materials in the process known as photosynthesis. In a growing tree, the carbon is 'locked up' in the tree's timber.

Since carbon dioxide is one of the 'greenhouse gases' that promote global warming, the forests may help reduce the problem. Yet the amount of carbon dioxide that is soaked up by ancient, natural rainforest is still debated. While the young forest trees are growing, old trees are dying and decaying, and so a well-established forest may release as much carbon as it absorbs.

Newly-planted forests are a different case, because the rate of growth, and therefore carbon 'lock-up', greatly exceeds the rate of decay and carbon release. On the basis of this theory, companies in the USA and other developed countries are now spending millions of dollars on planting forests in tropical countries as a way of soaking up some of the carbon dioxide generated by their own activities.

Rainforest trees and climbing plants act as photosynthesis factories, using the energy of sunlight to turn carbon dioxide and water into carbohydrate foods to sustain their own growth. In the process they absorb carbon dioxide from the atmosphere, and release oxygen.

Releasing the carbon

While planting trees may help store carbon, burning rainforest certainly does the opposite, releasing it back into the atmosphere. In 1998, for example, 9 million hectares of rainforest were destroyed by fire, releasing more than 1 billion tonnes of carbon dioxide.

Such fires have always been part of the rainforest cycle, and in natural forest the carbon released by fire is eventually absorbed by the young trees that grow in the scorched clearings. But in recent years many fires have been started deliberately to clear the land, so new trees cannot grow. Some of the released carbon may be absorbed by crops grown on the cleared land, but no one knows how much – or for how long.

In Brazil, a patch of rainforest is burned to make way for a soya plantation. Burning reverses the process of storing carbon, releasing it back into the atmosphere as carbon dioxide. There, as one of the principal greenhouse gases, it traps heat and contributes to global warming.

What other value do rainforests have?

Even though they cover only five per cent of the Earth's land area, the rainforests support more than half of all its species of plants and animals, and over two-thirds of the species that live on land. So the rainforests' survival is vital to a huge range of living things. Many of these are still virtually unknown to science; they have never been properly studied, their role in the web of life is unknown, and many do not even have scientific names.

Some products of the rainforest – such as wood, minerals, foods, rubber, rattan – have an economic value that is already being exploited, whether sustainably or wastefully. Other products may be sources of valuable foods or medicines that have never been discovered, and they could be lost for ever if the trees are cut down.

In the long run, though, the rainforests' importance goes beyond simple economics. It is hard to put a cash value

A heliconia flower provides a burst of vivid colour amid the greenery of the Colombian cloud forest – a glorious example of the beauty we risk losing.

on the beauty of a hummingbird or a morpho butterfly. And it is even more difficult to work out the exact worth of a living wilderness to a world jammed ever more tightly into cities and suburbs. As the planet becomes more crowded, wild places are becoming rarer. The rarer they get, the more we need to know that they are still out there.

Dawn rises over an untouched area of rainforest in northern Malaysia, near the border with Thailand.

DEBATE – Should poor nations try to develop their rainforest lands?

- Yes. For centuries the developed nations have been cutting down their own temperate woodlands to boost development. By exploiting their own resources, the rainforest nations are only following their example.
- No. There are real differences between rainforest and temperate woodland. The soil in most rainforest regions is not rich enough to support crops for long, and cutting down the trees simply risks creating a scrubby desert.

Forest diversity

Nobody knows how many species of animals there are on Earth. Well over one million species have been scientifically described, named and catalogued, and this certainly includes nearly all the larger, more conspicuous creatures like birds, mammals and reptiles. But how many unknown species of smaller, less obvious animals remain undiscovered among the trees of the tropical rainforests? Judging by the number of unknown creatures found each year, the named species are only a fraction of the total. In some samples from the rainforest canopy, an astonishing 90% of the insect species are new to science. So some researchers estimate that there may be up to 10 million insect species alone, plus countless molluscs, worms and similar creatures. And most of them live in the rainforest.

Why Are Rainforests Being Cut Down?

For thousands of years people have benefited from the rainforests without destroying them. Over the past century, though, the forests have been disappearing. The reasons for their loss are many and varied, but most come down to a single factor: growing human pressure to exploit their land and resources.

NO ONE DOUBTS that tropical rainforests are being cut down, or that the rate of loss is worrying. According to United Nations figures, about 14 million hectares of tropical forest – an area slightly bigger than England – were lost globally each year between 1980 and 1990, the most recent period for which agreed figures are available. The rate seems to have slowed a little over the next five years, but it may have risen again since 1995, partly as a result of a series of disastrous forest fires in Indonesia and Amazonia.

Local losses

The regional figures for rainforest loss make worrying reading. West Africa has seen nearly 75% of its rainforest vanish in the last 50 years; the figure rises to more than 90% in some countries, including Nigeria. In Asia, losses between 1990 and 1995 were estimated at 1.1% a year.

A satellite photograph shows how loggers are cutting their way into an area of Brazilian rainforest (dark green) and destroying it.

What lies behind the destruction?

One factor that often gets forgotten is technological advance. A hundred years ago, it took several men with axes more than a day to cut down a single large rainforest tree. Moving the felled timber was equally difficult: one observer estimated that it took loggers in Gabon an afternoon's work to shift a single trunk a mere 80m.

All that changed with the invention of chainsaws in the 1920s, the development of tractors that could pull several logs at once, and the use of trucks to haul the timber out of the forests. Within a few years it became possible to clear forest faster and over larger areas than had ever been the case before.

A workman employed by illegal loggers on the Indonesian island of Kalimantan (Borneo) cuts planks from a hardwood tree.

What is the point of clearing the forest?

As the new tools gradually spread around the world, people in developing countries started using them to exploit valuable forest resources. The most obvious of these was – and is – timber. The wealthy countries of the developed world provide a huge market for tropical hardwoods, and timber exports to these countries increased 16 times between 1950 and the 1990s. Logging companies grew rich on the trade. Governments backed them because the timber earned precious foreign currency, such as American dollars, to pay for technology and economic development.

The timber trade is still flourishing. Even so, logging itself accounts for only a relatively small part of forest loss – about 20 per cent, according to a United Nations estimate. Much more is being felled to clear the land for farming.

Trucks and bulldozers negotiate the slopes of a tin mine dug out of cleared rainforest land in Rondonia state, Brazil.

In some places governments have backed schemes to set up large estates on cleared land. In Asia, for example, many rubber and oil palm plantations have been created in this way. Elsewhere, the idea has been to provide smallholdings for landless peasants. In the 1950s the Brazilian government promised to open up part of the Amazon Basin as 'a land without men for men without land', conveniently overlooking the hundreds of thousands of indigenous forest peoples who were already living there.

Rainforest is also cut down to make way for mining operations designed to extract valuable minerals like oil, uranium and gold from the earth. Like timber, these minerals can be exported to rich industrial nations, earning the money to build roads and cities.

Over the past 20 years, huge tracts of Indonesian forest have been destroyed by fires, many started deliberately. The cleared land is often used for agricultural projects like this oil-palm plantation.

Is the forest clearance properly planned?

Much of the forest clearance is uncontrolled. A common pattern has developed in many different regions. A logging or oil-exploration company drives tracks through virgin forest for their own purposes. Land-hungry settlers then follow in their wake, using the new roads to get access to areas that they previously could not have reached. Then they use slash-and-burn techniques to clear a patch of land and plant it with crops.

For the first couple of years the land produces a good crop. Then, as the nutrients in the soil are used up, the yield declines. Before long the incomers are reduced to near-starvation. Often there are clashes with local indigenous peoples, who have learned to make food grow in the forest by regularly shifting cultivation in a way that the incomers cannot do, for there are just too many of them. Usually it is the native peoples who suffer. Sometimes they are attacked and driven out by the settlers. More often they fall victim to unfamiliar diseases, to which they have no natural immunity.

Why are settlers colonizing the forests?

There are many reasons why people seek out a new life in the forests. There is widespread hunger and poverty in the developing world, and little or no state welfare. This drives people to desperate measures. In many of the affected countries, an unjust distribution of the available farmland has put huge estates into the hands of a few very wealthy landowners, leaving little for the poorer citizens.

Above all, though, there is the relentless increase in the human population. As human numbers soar and the cities of the developing world expand and fill to overflowing, the rainforests seem to provide a way out. City people see them as a gigantic sponge that can soak up the surplus population. But the forests were never suitable places to settle, and by cutting them down the newcomers create not fertile agricultural plots, but a barren wilderness.

DEBATE – Should the sale of tropical hardwoods be banned?

- Yes. The hardwood trees are the backbone of the rainforests, and some take a century or more to reach their full height. They are currently being destroyed much faster than they can be replaced.
- No. The poor countries in which the trees grow desperately need the money that the trade brings in, to feed their people and pay their debts. With careful management, it should be possible to harvest the trees sustainably.

The shanty towns of cities like Manaus in Brazil are crowded with people who are eager to move into the forests in search of a better life.

Fire is a natural part of life in a rainforest, but fires like this one in Brazil are started deliberately to clear the land.

Are forests being destroyed by accidental fires?

Fire is nothing new in rainforests. As long as the forests have existed, natural blazes started by lightning strikes have destroyed trees and cleared patches of land. In the past such local fires did little harm. They usually burned themselves out quite quickly, thanks to the dampness of the soil, and they even played a part in helping new trees grow.

But over the past 20 years huge areas of forest, particularly in Indonesia, have been reduced to ashes by travelling walls of flame. As you would expect, the damage has been worst in years of drought, which themselves seem to be getting more common. But the problem has been made much worse by deliberate burning. The firestarters' aim is usually to clear land for development, or else to cover up evidence of illegal logging. So although some of the fires are undoubtedly accidental, others are part of the relentless drive to exploit and colonize the forests.

Burning the forest

The effects of the forest fires in Indonesia have been horrendous, and not just for Indonesia itself, where 2.4 million hectares of forest were burned in 1997 alone. Eventually this forest may recover, unless the land is cleared for other uses, but the fires caused other problems.

The smoke drifted into neighbouring countries, notably Singapore and Malaysia, causing an estimated $9 billion in damage to public health, agriculture, transport and tourism. And the effects may be lasting: smoke pollution is blamed for contributing to the Asian brown cloud, a band of haze some 3 km thick that now hangs permanently over much of southern Asia. Much of this pollution is being caused by vehicle exhausts and domestic fires, but the enormous forest fires do not help.

What Do We Risk By Destroying Rainforests?

Rainforests are incredibly rich in animals and plants, but they are also easy to destroy. Once the trees go, so does much of the life they shelter. The knock-on effects are often catastrophic for the peoples who already live in the forest, but even individuals far away may suffer from an increased risk of changes in the world's climate.

THE FIRST RISK involved in cutting down rainforest is what scientists call 'environmental degradation'. The richness of the forest disappears, to be replaced by scrub. With the tree cover gone, a downward spiral is quickly set in motion. Once they are no longer protected from the sunlight, the lower-growing plants dry out, and as they die the amount of water in the atmosphere above the forest declines further. According to one estimate, as much as half the moisture in the Amazon Basin is produced by plants as they transpire, or release water from their leaves.

In an intact rainforest, the minerals and nutrients needed to make the vegetation grow are endlessly recycled within the living plants, but once the trees come down these vital assets rapidly drain away into rivers and are lost to the area for good. Even the soil itself tends to wash away. One study in the Cauca Valley in Colombia, South America, found that, in the wake of deforestation, 40 tonnes of soil were lost from each hectare of the newly bare slopes in just 10 months. With no soil, new plants cannot take root, and the terrain rapidly becomes a wasteland.

What are the risks for wildlife?

The rainforest trees are disappearing at the rate of almost 400 sq. km each day – an area the size of Washington. And with them are going many of the animals, plants and tiny micro-organisms that make up the forest biosphere. The dangers are all the greater because of the sheer variety of living things the forests shelter. The figures can be startling. Over 2000 varieties of fish have been identified in the Amazon Basin – more than in the Atlantic Ocean. A 10-hectare plot of rainforest in Borneo can contain over 700 species of tree – the same number as the entire USA. A single rainforest tree in Peru was found to contain 43 different types of ant, as many as there are in all of Britain.

As a result, losing rainforest means losing life forms on a huge scale. Nobody knows for sure how many different species the world's rainforests contain, so estimates of the rate at which they are being lost are only inspired guesses. Even so, figures put forward suggesting that 2800 species might be going each year – nearly eight per day – give some idea of the scale of the crisis. Scientists currently estimate that one in ten of the world's tree species, one in eight of its plants and birds, and up to a quarter of its mammals are at some risk of dying out from loss of their wild habitat. The great majority of these threatened species live in the world's tropical rainforests.

The orang-utans of Indonesia and Malaysia are among the animals at risk of extinction as their rainforest habitat is destroyed.

Great tracts of forest in Madagascar have been reduced to barren land by soil erosion after forest clearance.

This periwinkle from the Madagascan rainforests provides a vital ingredient for the treatment of childhood leukemia.

Why does deforestation threaten medical research?

One area where species loss in the rainforests might hit particularly hard is medicine. Over millions of years the forest trees and other plants have developed chemical defences to protect themselves from the animals, birds and insects that prey on their leaves, seeds and fruit. In response, the insects in particular have developed chemical armouries of their own, often as defences against the poisons contained in particular plant species.

The result of this relentless struggle for survival is that the forests have become natural storehouses of drugs. Some forest plants are rich dispensaries of toxins, which although poisonous have great medicinal value. Scientists are only starting to explore the huge potential of these plants. Fewer than one in 100 have so far been tested, even though more than 100 pharmaceutical companies in the USA alone are engaged in plant research projects.

Yet the results have already been dramatic. According to some estimates, more than 120 prescription drugs now commonly available in doctors' surgeries and hospitals came originally from plant-derived sources. The US National Cancer Institute estimates that, of over 3000 plants known to help against cancer, 70 per cent come only from the world's rainforests.

How does deforestation threaten human societies?

People also suffer directly from the loss of the forests. The indigenous forest peoples are in the front line of casualties, and they have certainly suffered most from the exploitation of their homelands.

Today there are probably fewer than 250 000 indigenous forest people surviving in the Amazon Basin, where once there were several millions. The squeeze is becoming tighter as the outside world presses ever more closely on the remaining forest lands, making traditional cultures hard to maintain.

The lifestyles of indigenous people like this Panga tribesman from New Guinea are under threat as their living space shrinks.

The people who live around the forests are much more numerous; their numbers are put at more than 300 million worldwide. They also have much to lose, for they have always depended on the forest for many necessities of life, including food, building materials and medicinal plants. Above all they rely on the forest for firewood: in many developing countries, the fuel the trees provide supplies three-quarters of household energy needs for cooking and heating.

Traditional industries connected with the forests are also at risk if the trees are cut down. These include rattan gathering, rubber-tapping from wild rainforest trees, and even logging. Nigeria, which used to export hardwoods on a large scale, can now no longer meet its own needs and has become an importer.

Like many rainforest people, these Cofan in Ecuador have tried to adapt to the outside world. But the cities provide limited opportunities, and they have been reduced to selling curios to tourists on the streets.

Does tree loss affect water supplies?

People living further afield may also be badly affected by deforestation if they live on the great rivers that drain the forests. Over a billion people depend on the water that flows from tropical forests, both for drinking and for crop irrigation. If a forest is felled, it no longer acts as a sponge to soak up rain and gradually release it. So the people who live downstream risk being subjected to alternating droughts and floods as the water from tropical storms flows unchecked over bare earth.

A further danger comes from soil eroded from the former forest lands, either as a result of deforestation or because of large-scale industrial projects. This is carried down the rivers as silt, killing fish, blocking dams, and contaminating irrigation schemes and reservoirs of drinking water.

This stream in New Guinea has been polluted by silt spilling out from a mining operation in the mountains, contaminating a vital water supply for the people living further downstream.

DEBATE - Can rainforest land be put to better use?

- Yes. Most rainforests grow in poor parts of the world where local people barely have enough to live on. The quickest way to increase their standard of living is to exploit all available resources, and that means the land, its timber and minerals.
- No. If the tree cover is cut down, all the life it shelters soon goes. For a few years some people could make a lot of money, but once the forest's assets have been stripped, all that will be left is a wasteland of no benefit to anyone.

The loss of tropical rainforest could have unpredictable effects on the global climate. When forests are burned, the carbon from the incinerated trees is released as carbon dioxide. This may be increasing carbon dioxide levels in the atmosphere, which contributes to global warming.

The rise in global temperature is certainly happening, although scientists still argue over the contribution of deforestation, and how it may affect worldwide wind patterns and the transfer of heat around the globe. Much about forest loss remains unknown, but few are predicting benefits that could outweigh its potentially disastrous consequences.

If deforestation does contribute to global warming, the destruction of the rainforests may even be affecting creatures like these polar bears, whose icy Arctic habitat has shrunk by up to 15 per cent over the past 30 years.

The death of Chico Mendes

Shortly before dusk on 22 December 1988 a 44-year-old rubber-tapper named Chico Mendes stepped out of his house in the Brazilian state of Acre. Two men with guns were waiting for him outside. Shot in the chest, he died instantly.

Mendes was a leader of the rubber tappers who, for more than a century, had been earning a living by draining latex, the raw material of rubber, from rainforest trees. This does no permanent harm to the trees, and it once provided a living for up to half a million people. In recent years, however, their livelihood had been threatened by developers seeking to build roads and establish cattle ranches in the area. Chico Mendes helped organize non-violent action in protest against the destruction of the forest.

Mendes's work for the forest won him fame and honours abroad, but it also made him powerful enemies at home. In Acre alone, more than 50 people had been killed in the previous 13 years, on the orders of people who hoped to grow rich from cutting down the forest. Mendes himself survived half a dozen attempts on his life before he was finally killed. Ironically, he achieved more by his death than he had ever done when alive. The murder drew international attention to his cause, and the state was forced to take action against his killers.

A rubber tapper extracts latex sustainably on the Chico Mendes Reserve in Brazil.

Can The Rainforests Be Saved?

If the present rate of loss continues, all the world's remaining rainforests could disappear within a century. Yet there are ways in which they can be put to greater economic use without being destroyed. Their future may be secured by establishing central reserves, fringed by areas where the forest's products can be harvested in a sustainable way.

Ecotourist schemes such as this walkway through the rainforest canopy in East Kalimantan, Indonesia, offer one way of funding rainforest conservation.

THE RAINFORESTS OF the world are being destroyed for two main reasons. Technological progress has made it relatively easy to cut the trees down and haul them out of the forest, and people from outside the forests are exploiting other forest resources such as land and minerals. They can be saved, but only if politicians and other people in power decide to protect them.

Some people would like to keep the rainforests exactly as they are, and in an ideal world that might be best. But there are so many pressures on the forests that their preservation in totality is unlikely. The most practical way forward is a conservation strategy that allows some development to provide a living for as many people as possible – but without destroying the fabric of the forest.

How can this be achieved?

One thing that is certain is that some core areas of rainforest will have to be preserved untouched. This is essential if their precious wildlife is to survive, as well as the lifestyles of indigenous forest peoples. In today's crowded world, that means setting them aside as wilderness reserves, or indigenous territories controlled by the people who have traditionally lived in them.

Many such protected areas already exist. On one count, there are about 2000 of them in tropical countries, covering a total area of more than 2 million sq. km, although only about a third currently contain rainforest. Those that do are not always properly policed to prevent poaching or illegal logging, but at least the reserves exist.

Around these central regions, where the interests of nature must come first, the outer rim of the forest could be exploited in ways that do not inflict lasting damage. There are many renewable forest resources that have been harvested, often for hundreds or even thousands of years, and with careful management these could be put to greater use.

Latex has been tapped in the Amazon for over 100 years. It spawned a huge economic boom in the late nineteenth century, before the seeds were transported by the British to Malaysia where they became the foundation of a thriving rubber plantation industry. Then there is rattan, the stem of a climbing plant that grows naturally in the forest. Rattan is the raw material for a multi-million-dollar basket-making and furniture trade.

As for foods, the rainforest has already given the world such favourites as bananas, vanilla, coffee and the cacao beans from which chocolate is made. Yet it also contains hundreds of other fruits eaten by indigenous peoples that have never been commercially exploited. Add in gums, nuts, palm oil and medicinal plants, and it soon becomes obvious just how valuable the forest harvest could be. One estimate suggests that the sustainable collection of natural resources in the rainforests of Peru could yield as much as $6800 US per hectare, compared with just $150 from ranching and $1000 from logging.

One encouraging sign is that Brazil has recently announced plans to give indigenous peoples control of 20 per cent of the Amazonian rainforest, which they will then be able to exploit in a sustainable fashion. The plans also include provision to turn another five per cent of the forest into a nature reserve.

A worker harvests cacao pods on a plantation in Ghana. The beans inside the pods are used to make chocolate.

Will this strategy work?

One problem with this rosy picture is that sustainable management, which allows the forest to be used and reused for generations to come, involves patient and controlled use of its resources. The forest products must be exploited on a scale that is small enough to allow trees and plants to regrow. Yet people seeking to make quick profits will always be tempted to strip everything at once, with disastrous results.

Another problem involves access. To harvest forest products sustainably,

workers must still be able to reach them, and that means clearing roads and tracks. These in turn open up the forest to incomers who may have no concern for its long-term survival.

Such problems can be overcome, but only if governments are watchful and put enough local wardens and rangers in the protected areas to make sure that the rules are obeyed. Policing the rainforest is an expensive job, and a heavy drain on the budgets of the generally poor developing nations that preserve most of the forest that remains.

How can people in the West help?

There are ways in which people of all ages in industrial countries can help. We can buy goods – rattan baskets or decorations, for instance – from the specialist shops that import from developing countries. We can do our best to check that any hardwood furniture or house fittings we buy come from sustainably managed forests.

Most importantly, we can support politicians and other powerful people and organizations that show they are aware of the problem, because these are the people who can make a difference. We can encourage governments to contribute financially, whether by granting aid to countries that are seeking to save the forests, or by cancelling their debts. We can also join conservation organizations like the Rainforest Foundation and Friends of the Earth, that campaign to preserve the forest. Many of these organizations encourage younger members – and the younger you are, the more you have to lose if the rainforests disappear.

For millions of years the world's rainforests looked after themselves, but they will need all the help we can give them if they are to have a future.

In Cameroon, local students learn about their forest through an environmental education project.

Cloud swirls through a stand of unspoiled rainforest in Malaysia. Such sights could be preserved for future generations – but only if we encourage our political leaders to make the environment a priority.

REFERENCE

THE WORLD'S RAINFOREST COUNTRIES

(Listed by continent, showing the percentage of total forested area classed as rainforest. Some small countries and island groups have been omitted.)

AFRICA
Equatorial Guinea	100%
Gabon	99%
Liberia	99%
Congo	95%
Democratic Republic of Congo	82%
Uganda	78%
Côte d'Ivoire	63%
Cameroon	61%
Ghana	47%
Sierra Leone	40%
Madagascar	34%
Guinea	28%
Central African Republic	23%
Nigeria	22%
Togo	19%
Angola	9%
Sudan	7%
Benin	5%
Kenya	1%
Mozambique	1%
Tanzania	1%

ASIA
Brunei	100%
Singapore	100%
Malaysia	94%
Indonesia	88%
The Philippines	81%
Bangladesh	63%
Myanmar	35%
East Timor	33%
Vietnam	26%
Laos	25%
Thailand	23%
Nepal	19%
Sri Lanka	18%
India	13%
Cambodia	7%

AUSTRALASIA
Polynesia	100%
Papua New Guinea	80%
Australia	2%

CENTRAL AMERICA AND THE CARIBBEAN
Trinidad & Tobago	100%
Puerto Rico	93%
Jamaica	84%
Dominica	79%
Haiti	75%
Grenada	71%
Martinique	68%
Panama	66%
Guadeloupe	62%
Costa Rica	61%
St Lucia	61%
Dominican Republic	59%
Honduras	53%
Belize	42%
Guatemala	41%
Cuba	32%
Bahamas	29%
Antigua	22%
Mexico	9%
El Salvador	7%

AREAS OF FOREST COVER LOST EACH YEAR IN SELECTED RAINFOREST LANDS, 1990-2000

(in square kilometres)

SOUTH AMERICA

French Guiana	100%
Peru	86%
Colombia	84%
Brazil	76%
Guyana	74%
Ecuador	60%
Surinam	58%
Venezuela	51%
Bolivia	32%
Argentina	4%
Paraguay	1%

(Source: Food and Agriculture Organization of the United Nations, 2000.)

Brazil	23 090
Indonesia	13 120
Dem. Rep. of the Congo	5320
Myanmar	5170
Nigeria	3980
Peru	2690
Côte d'Ivoire	2650
Malaysia	2370
Cameroon	2220
Venezuela	2180
Colombia	1900
Bolivia	1610
Ecuador	1370
Angola	1240
Ghana	1200
Madagascar	1170
Nicaragua	1170
Papua New Guinea	1130
Thailand	1120
Uganda	910
The Philippines	890
Liberia	760
Honduras	590
Cambodia	560
Guatemala	540
Laos	530
Panama	520
Vietnam	520

(Source: Food and Agriculture Organization of the United Nations, 2000. Figures include all types of forest in each country.)

COUNTRIES WITH THE GREATEST REMAINING AREA OF RAINFOREST

(by continent, in square kilometres)

AFRICA

Dem. Rep. of Congo	1 108 700
Gabon	216 100
Congo	209 600
Cameroon	145 500
Angola	62 800
Central African Republic	52 700
Côte d'Ivoire	44 800
Sudan	43 100
Madagascar	39 900
Liberia	34 500
Uganda	32 700
Ghana	29 800
Nigeria	29 700
Guinea	19 400
Equatorial Guinea	17 500

ASIA

Indonesia	923 900
Malaysia	181 300
Myanmar	120 500
India	83 300
The Philippines	46 900
Thailand	34 000
Laos	31 400
Vietnam	25 500
Bangladesh	8400
Cambodia	6500

AUSTRALASIA

Papua New Guinea	244 800
Australia	30 900

CENTRAL AMERICA AND THE CARIBBEAN

Mexico	49 700
Honduras	28 500
Nicaragua	24 300
Panama	19 000
Costa Rica	12 000
Guatemala	11 700

SOUTH AMERICA

Brazil	4 133 700
Peru	560 800
Colombia	416 600
Venezuela	252 500
Bolivia	169 800
Guyana	124 900
Surinam	81 900
French Guiana	79 300
Ecuador	63 300
Argentina	13 900

(*Source: FAO, 2000*)

RAINFOREST LANDS THAT HAVE KEPT MOST FOREST COVER

(as percentage of original forest)

Surinam	92%
French Guiana	92%
Guyana	82%
Colombia	64%
Venezuela	59%
Peru	57%
Brazil	42%
Papua New Guinea	40%
Ecuador	37%
Belize	35%
Panama	35%
Gabon	32%

(Source: World Resources Institute, 2002)

RAINFOREST COUNTRIES WITH THE HIGHEST PLANT BIODIVERSITY

(estimated number of higher plant species in forests)

Brazil	36 000
Colombia	34 000
Indonesia	18 000
Venezuela	15 000
Peru	13 000
Ecuador	12 000
Malaysia	8000
Papua New Guinea	7000

(Source: World Resources Institute, 2002)

LARGEST WOOD-PRODUCING RAINFOREST COUNTRIES

(in millions of cubic metres)

Brazil	269
Indonesia	185
Nigeria	115
Malaysia	53

(Source: World Commission on Forests and Sustainable Development, 1999)

GLOSSARY

blowpipe A long, hollow tube, usually the stem of a rainforest plant, from which pellets or darts can be fired by blowing.

bromeliad One of a family of spiny-leaved plants, the *Bromeliaceae*, that includes many epiphytes (see below).

carbon An element that can combine with many other elements to make the complex molecules of life.

carbon dioxide (CO_2) A gas formed from carbon and oxygen, released by breathing animals and by burning carbon-rich fossil fuels and trees.

cassava A root plant, also known as manioc, that is an important food source in the tropics.

cold-blooded animal An animal that must bask in the sun or seek shade to maintain its body temperature.

condensation The process by which water vapour in the atmosphere turns into liquid droplets.

decomposition The rotting process by which leaf litter and other debris is broken down into simpler substances.

ecosystem An area or system containing living things linked together by a web of relationships.

environmental degradation The breakdown of an ecosystem so that it can no longer renew itself, and is replaced by less productive growth.

epiphyte A plant with no roots in the soil that grows on another plant, but without taking nourishment from its host as parasites do.

erosion The wearing away of soil and rock by water or wind.

fungi The plural of 'fungus'; any of a group of organisms that absorb food through a network of fine threads, reproducing by spores often carried in fruiting bodies that include mushrooms.

greenhouse gases The various gases, including carbon dioxide and methane, that trap the Sun's heat in Earth's atmosphere; a surplus of such gases may be causing global warming.

habitat An animal or plant's natural living space.

hardwood trees Any of a variety of trees whose tough, often resinous wood is prized by woodworkers.

hibernate To pass the winter in a state resembling sleep, with many bodily functions slowed down – a rare condition in the rainforest, which has no winter.

humus Soil enriched with nutrients from decaying animals or plants.

hunter-gatherers People who live by a combination of hunting animals and gathering wild fruits, nuts, berries etc.

immunity The body's natural defences against infection.

indigenous peoples Native people who have lived for a long time in a given area.

irrigation The channelling of water to promote crop growth.

latex The sticky white sap of the rubber tree, used to make rubber.

leaf litter The layer of dead leaves and other debris on the forest floor.

liana Any of a variety of climbing or hanging plants rooted in the ground, and often found in rainforests.

mangrove Tropical plants that grow in dense thickets along coasts, often with their roots in the sea water.

montane Refers to plants that grow in mountainous regions.

nutrients Anything that provides nourishment for living things, whether from decaying plants and animals (organic nutrients) or from minerals in rocks (inorganic nutrients).

organic Involving life forms, whether living or dead, based on carbon (all life on Earth is carbon-based).

pharmaceutical Involved in the production of drugs for medicine.

photosynthesis The process by which plants make sugars from carbon dioxide and water, using the energy of sunlight.

plantation An estate on which trees or crops are planted and harvested for sale.

rattan The tough stems of climbing palms, used for wickerwork or as canes; the rainforests' second most valuable wild crop, after timber.

renewable resources Resources that are only harvested at a rate that permits them to regrow.

root-mat The spreading, criss-crossing roots of some rainforest trees, that soak up every available drop of moisture.

secondary-growth forest The jumble of vegetation that grows when primary, or first-growth forest is cut down, allowing the sun's rays to reach the forest floor.

slash-and-burn cultivation A farming technique that involves clearing an area of forest and burning the vegetation to release the nutrients it contains, making the soil beneath fertile for a time.

smallholding A small plot of land farmed by a single owner or family.

sustainable management The use of land in such a way that the resources it contains are not used up but continue to be available to subsequent generations.

symbiotic relationship A mutual-assistance relationship between two different animal or plant species, that benefits both.

temperate Belonging to the regions of the world midway between the Equator and the poles, where temperatures are generally less extreme.

transpiration The loss of moisture from leaves and other plant surfaces as a result of evaporation.

tree canopy The roof of leaves that the highest trees extend over undisturbed rainforest.

understorey The lower level of smaller trees and shrubs that lies below the forest canopy.

water cycle The process by which water falls to earth as rain, evaporates, rises into the sky as water vapour, and then once more turns into rain.

FURTHER INFORMATION

BOOKS
Non-Fiction
The Last Rain Forests, ed. Mark Collins (Mitchell Beazley World Conservation Atlas, 1990)

Mysteries of the Rain Forest by Linda Gamlin and Anuschka de Rohan (Reader's Digest, 1996)

The Fate of the Forest by Susanna Hecht and Alexander Cockburn (Penguin Books, 1990)

In the Rainforest by Catherine Caufield (Pan, 1986)

The Tapir's Morning Bath: Solving the Mysteries of the Tropical Rain Forest by Elizabeth Royte (Mariner Books, 2002)

Tropical Nature by Adrian Forsyth and Kenneth Miyata (Scribner, 1987)

The Decade of Destruction by Adrian Cowell (Hodder & Stoughton Educational, 1990)

The Forest and the Sea by Marston Bates (Vintage, 1973)

Fiction
Green Mansions by W.H. Hudson (Dover, 1989; first published in 1904)

FILMS
The Burning Season (directed by John Frankenheimer, starring Raul Julia and Sonia Braga, 1994)

Medicine Man (directed by John McTiernan, starring Sean Connery, 1992)

VIDEOS
Baka: People of the Rain Forest (DJA River Films for Channel 4, 1987)

Really Wild Animals – Totally Tropical Rain Forest (narrated by Dudley Moore, 1994)

WEBSITES
www.wrm.org.uy
Website of the World Rainforest Movement. Provides information on deforestation, action alerts, news of campaigns etc.

www.rainforestweb.org
Website of the US-based Rainforest Action Network – an umbrella site for groups campaigning to save the forests.

http://earthtrends.wri.org
Website run by the World Resources Institute. Provides detailed statistics on forest clearance.

www.rainforestfoundationuk.org
Website of the Rainforest Foundation, the charity set up by the singer Sting, among others, to work for the preservation of the forests.

www.panda.org
Website of the organization once known as the World Wildlife Fund, now 'WWF'. Click on 'Forests' for rainforest news.

www.survival-international.org
Website of Survival International, which campaigns for the rights of indigenous peoples.

www.greenpeace.org
Website of Greenpeace, which campaigns on environmental issues.

ORGANIZATIONS

The bodies listed below are all concerned with the survival of the rainforests and the welfare of the people and animals that live in them:

Rainforest Foundation (UK)
City Cloisters,
196 Old Street,
London EC1V 9FR
Tel: 020 7251 6345
Email: rainforestuk@rainforestuk.com

World Rainforest Movement
WRM Northern Office,
1C The Fosseway Business Centre,
Stratford Road,
Moreton-in-Marsh GL56 9NQ
Tel: 01608 652895
Email: wrm@gn.apc.org

WWF-UK
Panda House,
Weyside Park,
Godalming,
Surrey GU7 1XR
Tel: 01483 426444

Friends of the Earth
26-28 Underwood Street,
London N1 7JQ
Tel: 020 7490 1555

Greenpeace
Canonbury Villas,
London, N1 2PN
Tel: 020 7865 8100
Email: info@uk.greenpeace.org

Living Earth
4 Great James Street,
London WC1N 3DB
Tel: 020 7440 9750
Email: info@livingearth.org.uk

Survival International
6 Charterhouse Buildings,
London EC1M 7ET
Tel: 020 7687 8700
Email: info@survival-international.org

INDEX